WORLD IN CRISIS

THE RACE TO FEED THE
HUNGRY

Mary Colson

rosen publishing's
rosen
central

NEW YORK

Published in 2015 by The Rosen Publishing Group, Inc.
29 East 21st Street
New York, NY 10010

Produced for Rosen by Calcium Creative Ltd.
Editor for Calcium Creative Ltd.: Sarah Eason
Designer: Paul Myerscough
Picture research: Rachel Blount

Library of Congress Cataloging-in-Publication Data

Colson, Mary.
The race to feed the hungry/by Mary Colson, first edition.
    p. cm.—(World in crisis)
Includes bibliographical references and index.
ISBN 978-1-4777-7846-3 (library binding)
1. Hunger—Juvenile literature. 2. Food relief—Juvenile literature. 3. Social
action—Juvenile literature. I. Colson, Mary. II. Title.
HV696.F6 C65 2015
363.8—d23

Manufactured in Malaysia

Contents

A Global Problem

Hunger is the world's number one health risk. It kills more people every year than HIV/AIDS, malaria, and tuberculosis combined. The world's population is growing year by year. Unless we find a way to produce more food, more quickly, hunger will continue to kill millions of people in the poorest parts of the world.

More People, Less Food

There are currently 870 million people in the world who do not have enough to eat—and this number is growing. Population growth is out of control in many developing areas, such as Africa and India. Here, more and more children are being born each year, but with less and less food to feed them.

The Victims of Hunger

Children who cannot receive proper nourishment may be ill for as many as 160 days every year. Of 10.9 million child deaths across the globe every year, at least half—5 million—are the result of poor nutrition. Diseases such as measles and malaria can be made even worse by malnutrition. Roughly, the proportion of deaths in which malnutrition is considered the hidden cause are very much alike for diarrhea (61 percent), malaria (57 percent), pneumonia (52 percent), and measles (45 percent).

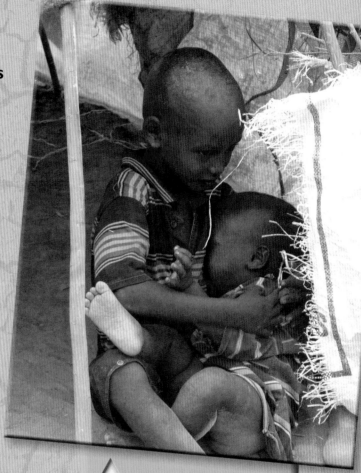

In developing countries, one in four children is underweight. Five million children under the age of five years old die every year from malnutrition.

More and Quicker

We cannot create more farmland, so in order to be able to feed the world's growing people, we need to be able to produce more food—but on the same amount of land, and much more quickly than we currently do. There is no time to waste in our race to find a solution to our growing food crisis.

Superfoods

Scientists are currently developing "supercrops." These are plants that can gather much more energy from the Sun, far more quickly than ordinary plants. This means they grow much larger, and much faster than the food crops we currently farm. By growing supercrops, farmers could grow twice as much food in a year, on the same amount of land, as they currently do.

Scientists are also looking into methods by which to create giant-sized forms of food. They are using genetic modification to alter the genes of many different foods, from fruits and vegetables, to eggs. Could these supersized foods be the solution to our growing food crisis?

One day, we may even see factories producing huge quantities of giant superfoods, such as supersized eggs, to help feed our growing population.

CHAPTER ONE

Why Do Some People Go Hungry?

There are many reasons why people go hungry. Poverty, war, a history of famine, overpopulation, climate change, crop failure, and political failure are just some of them. A country may be too poor to buy enough food for its people, while another may suffer from droughts or floods and not be able to grow sufficient food. In some places, there are simply too many mouths to feed and not enough food to go around.

Hunger or Famine?

For many millions of people all over the world, hunger means more than just an empty stomach. Hunger also means having to survive on less than the recommended 2,100 calories we need each day to lead a healthy, fulfilling life. By contrast, famine is a severe shortage of food that may be caused by natural or man-made events.

If crops fail, the consequences can be devastating. Food prices rise and people can go hungry.

The Price People Pay

Hunger and famine both lead to malnutrition, which is a condition in which people do not get enough healthy food. This causes the body to slow down its physical activities and mental processes. A hungry mind cannot concentrate; a starving body cannot run around and play. Malnutrition also damages the immune system, making people more vulnerable to illnesses or diseases. Severe hunger or famine among a group of people means that epidemics, where disease spreads rapidly, are common, leading to many deaths.

LOOK TO THE PAST

What would you do if you had many people to feed but little land or money? You would need to produce food that is easy to grow, nutritious, and filling. You might decide to focus all your time and energy on growing one crop, such as potatoes. This is what happened in Ireland until the disastrous summer of 1845 and the event that became known as the Irish Potato Famine. During 1845, an airborne fungus that had been carried to Ireland in the holds of ships from North America attacked Ireland's potato plants. Thousands of people starved, and thousands left the country to begin new lives elsewhere. Although a fungus caused the potato crop to fail, monocropping, or depending on only one crop, caused the famine. People now know that it is important to grow many kinds of crops so that if one crop fails, the others will still provide food.

With a global population of more than 8 billion, harvesting enough wheat and grain is essential to ensure the survival of people worldwide.

Is There a Global Food Shortage?

For decades, there has been an imbalance in food production. In the developed countries of the West, people have produced more food than they can eat, while people in Africa and other developing regions of the world have not produced enough food. In Europe in the 1980s, there were so-called "butter mountains" and "milk lakes" of surplus food that went to waste. However, by 2010, the world was consuming more food than it produced. This meant that food reserves around the world started to diminish and costs began to rise dramatically. The result for poor people now is that they spend an even greater amount of their incomes simply feeding themselves and their families. Why has the shortage of some foodstuffs happened?

The World's Bread Baskets

Wheat is one of the world's key crops, and Russia and the United States are the world's chief wheat-growing countries. Between them, if every harvest was at its best, these two countries could provide daily bread for every person around the world. However, a series of poor harvests has left world grain reserves dangerously low and the price of wheat has rocketed. The cost of a loaf of bread has already doubled in the past 10 years. Any further disruption to the wheat harvest through extreme weather would send the price even higher and trigger a major hunger crisis in developing countries.

Shortages and Riots

If food prices rise, poor people will have to spend even more of their income on food, which could lead to severe global problems. The United Nations (UN) warns that the food crisis is growing in the Middle East and Africa. Crops such as wheat, oats, and barley are yielding smaller global harvests. Only rice production is increasing. If the food supply chain collapses, it will not only be prices that rise—the number of people going hungry will soar, too. If this happens, widespread rioting could occur and even governments could be brought down, causing enormous political instability worldwide.

SCIENCE SOLUTIONS

Drought Proof

Scientists believe that we need to change what we farm, and how we farm it, in order to avoid a food supply crisis. Climate change means that "normal" weather patterns can no longer be depended on, so developing crops that are resistant to extreme weather is vital. Drought-resistant wheat is already being trialed across Africa.

Food riots are still happening today. This protest took place in Greece in 2012 as a result of austerity measures introduced by the Greek government in response to the financial crisis that began in 2008.

Hunger Map of the World

The International Food Policy Research Institute (IFPRI) has produced a list of the hungriest nations—the Global Hunger Index (GHI). The Index shows that two-thirds of the world's hungry live in just seven countries: Bangladesh, China, the Democratic Republic of the Congo, Ethiopia, India, Indonesia, and Pakistan. It ranks the poor African nation of Burundi as the most hunger-affected country in the world. Two-thirds of its 10 million population live below the level of income, known as the "poverty line" needed just to have the basic necessities of life, especially food.

A Hungry Continent

Africa is the hungriest continent on Earth, with one in four of its people failing to get enough to eat. Africa has already lost more than 7 million farmers to the HIV/AIDS disease. That is more than the total number of famers in Europe and North America. Without farmers, food production is falling rapidly. More than 23 million children in Africa go to school hungry every day. Hunger is rising by 2 percent every year in countries such as Angola, Mali, and Guinea.

Crisis in Asia

There are more than 570 million hungry people in Asia, the world's largest continent. Natural disasters, low employment rates, and the bad management of resources are part of the problem. More people suffer from hunger in the Indian state of Punjab than in both of the African countries Ethiopia and Sudan.

In some parts of the world, hunger rates are rising fast leaving many poor children starving and severely malnourished.

Desperately hungry Somali children and their mothers reach out for food aid at a refugee camp.

Hunger in the Americas

Even in the United States, almost 50 million people, including 16 million children, live in households that cannot always afford to eat. In Mexico, around 45 percent of its 118 million people face food shortages or hunger. In South America, nearly 10 million Peruvians suffer from hunger: that is nearly one-third of the population. There, as in so many countries around the world, it is the rural poor who suffer most.

COUNTDOWN!

With every failed harvest and increase in food prices, the number of hungry people rises. Other factors such as illness and disease affect the food production chain—and family life. In some parts of the world, children might lose both parents to diseases like malaria or HIV/AIDS and then struggle to feed themselves. Hunger does not affect only poor countries. For example, the UN Children's Fund estimates that nearly 600,000 children in Greece are living below the poverty line. The millions of people suffering all over the world can only go hungry for so long.

CHAPTER TWO

Causes of Hunger

The more fortunate people of the world live in countries that have a stable government and are rich in natural resources such as good-quality soil and fresh water.

Infrastructure

These countries have roads and railroads to transport food to people in villages, towns, and cities. In these countries, there are high employment rates, and people can afford to buy food. There are no conflicts, and health care and education are well funded. The weather is also fairly stable, and if there is a dry spell or it rains more than usual, the country can cope and has ways of managing food supplies. However, there are many people who do not live in such stable countries. This chapter will look at the key causes of hunger and find out why it is that some areas of the world are trapped in a devastating cycle of poverty and hunger.

People in remote communities, such as this one in the Philippines, grow their own food. If there is a famine, however, these villages can be difficult to reach.

Political Corruption

Some of the hungriest people in the world live in poor countries that are controlled by corrupt or inadequate governments. In these places, the wealth and resources are in the hands of a few people who live well while the rest of the population barely survives. Even food aid sent by charities overseas does not always get to those who need it. Sometimes, the food is taken by the government and sold to other countries for a profit.

LOOK TO THE PAST

In 1921, Russia was still recovering from the economic effects of World War I and the political upheaval of a violent revolution. A long drought had left the crops shriveled and dying. A year later, famine gripped the land. The Russian railroad system was old-fashioned and could not move food around the country efficiently. Charities and relief agencies from abroad sent food parcels, but they were not enough—6 million people starved.

Transportation Problems

A failure of food distribution is one of the biggest causes of hunger. Most of the world's hungry people live in remote rural places where there are few tracks or roads, and even fewer railroads. In these places, the transportation and communication infrastructure simply is not able to get enough food to where it is needed. The situation is slowly changing, but not quickly enough for hungry people in need of food.

The UN World Food Programme (WFP) is the world's largest food aid organization. It supplies thousands of starving people with food.

Failing Harvests and the Meat Feast

Three-quarters of all the world's hungry people live in the countryside, mainly in villages in Africa and Asia. These populations rely completely on their own crops— they have no alternative source of food. The UN estimates that around half of the world's hungry people are in small farming communities who survive on crops grown on "marginal land." This is land that is prone to natural disasters such as drought, flooding, or landslides. Marginal land is usually made up of poor-quality soil, so each year the crops grown on the land produce less food. If the harvest fails, everyone goes hungry. This can turn into widespread famine if a country has total harvest failure and cannot afford to buy and import grain from elsewhere.

Feeding the Rich

Another important factor in world hunger is how people in developed countries consume food. Many of us love to eat a hamburger or a juicy steak. However, the global meat production industry devours too many important resources.

Rearing and grazing cattle uses vast amounts of land and precious water, which could instead be used to grow crops.

SCIENCE SOLUTIONS

Chemical Change

Biotechnology, which involves changing living things to make new organic products, may provide an answer to the nutrition problem in some parts of the world. By altering the chemicals in plants, scientists could make those plants better able to resist pests, flooding, or drought. Scientists are also working on adding nutrients such as minerals and vitamins to basic foods such as rice and potatoes. This is called biofortification. However, much of this research is being carried out in Europe and North America, where the general public are concerned about scientists interfering with nature. Some worry that this Western concern may stop vital investment and delay potentially life-saving research.

Land where cattle graze takes up more than one-quarter of the entire planet's usable land surface. Crops grown to feed the cattle make up one-third of all arable land. From these crops, it takes an incredible 7 pounds (3 kilograms) of grain to produce 1 pound (0.5 kilograms) of beef. It also takes nearly 4 million gallons (15 million liters) of fresh water to produce 1 ton (0.9 metric ton) of meat. All these resources are needed to satisfy the meat-heavy Western diet, but the amounts are simply not sustainable with a growing world population. According to the UN, agricultural yields must increase by 60 percent by the middle of this century to feed the additional 2 billion people living on the planet.

When war occurs, many thousands of people can be affected. Displaced people flee to refugee camps in search of food and refuge.

Casualties of War

If you were in danger and had to leave your home suddenly, what would you decide to take with you? How much could you carry? Would you take enough food to last for a week, or even longer?

The Cost of Conflict

Since 1990, there have been many food crises caused by war. Conflict causes specific food problems because it displaces people, often forcing them away from land that may have been well managed and fertile. For nearly a decade, the Darfur region of Sudan in North Africa has endured a major food crisis. More than 1 million people have been displaced because of an ongoing conflict, and good farmland has fallen into disuse or been destroyed in the fighting.

A Worsening Crisis

The UN estimates that anywhere between 15 and 30 million people around the world have been displaced by war, nearly half of them under 18 years of age. That means that every single day, around 23,000 people leave their homes to seek protection elsewhere. Even more staggering is the fact that every 4.1 seconds someone in the world becomes a displaced person. Some of these people will leave not only their homes, but also their country. They will become refugees, fleeing across borders into other countries whose own people may be struggling with hunger themselves.

Hunger as a Weapon

Throughout history, wars and other conflicts have caused food shortages and hunger. Conflict upsets daily work routines, destroys land and crops, and stops people from earning a living. Even hunger itself can be used as a weapon. Destroying food stocks, placing land mines in fields, killing livestock, poisoning water supplies, and diverting food aid away from those in need are just some of the ways hunger becomes a part of war. If farmers abandon their crops, food production will fall fast, prices will rise, and hunger will soon follow.

The ongoing conflict in Sudan means that the UN Food Program is feeding more than 50,000 people. Continual supplies of food must be airlifted into the country to supply its starving people.

COUNTDOWN!

Food shortages that result from conflict can lead to years of food emergencies, even after the fighting has stopped. Today's conflicts in Syria and Mali are just the start of hunger problems that could take decades to resolve.

Food Insecurity

Many experts believe that food security is the single greatest challenge facing the world today. What is food security, and what factors can affect it?

A Fragile Food Balance

Food security means that a person has access all the time to enough nutritious food and clean water so he or she can maintain a healthy and active life. Developed countries have food security because they have money to buy any food they do not produce themselves. They also have transportation networks to distribute the food. However, in the developing world there is the opposite problem—food insecurity. This can be caused by events beyond anyone's control such as volcanic eruptions, floods, or other natural disasters. Food insecurity can also result from bad farming practices, poor management of resources, and mistaken government control.

The Poverty Trap

Hunger and poverty are two of the biggest threats to a nation's food security—and each threat encourages the other. Hunger can pave the road for even more significant poverty when it results in unhealthy people with low energy levels and possibly mental impairment. Hunger then makes it less likely that they can work and learn and this creates far more intense hunger. This situation traps millions of people all over the world, but what is being done to change it? What can governments and organizations do to ensure better food security for the world's most vulnerable people?

Although most people in developed countries have food security, the price of food has been steadily rising over recent years. A number of people on low incomes in developed countries now struggle to buy enough food for their families.

World Food Agreement

In 2009, the UN Food and Agriculture Organization (FAO) held an important conference, called the World Summit on Food Security. Scientists and representatives from all over the world gathered in Rome, Italy, to discuss ways of improving food security for all people. Providing better energy supplies to developing countries was high on the agenda. Without enough energy, food cannot be processed or transported to where it is needed.

In China, farmers work hard in the rice fields but they get very little money for the crop. They struggle to survive on the $800 they earn per year.

LOOK TO THE PAST

In the 1950s, the leader of China, Mao Tse-Tung, tried to guide his country into a new era of economic success. He wanted China to move away from farming toward manufacturing iron and steel instead. New laws banned people from owning farms, and millions of farm laborers were ordered to work in steel and iron factories, leaving few people to tend to the crops. The resulting famine killed an estimated 40 million people. Mao did not think about securing the food supply, and the Chinese people suffered the tragic consequences.

> Every year, locusts cause millions of dollars of damage to crops and have a devastating effect on the supply of food to people in affected countries.

Climate Change

Weather patterns across the world are becoming increasingly unpredictable and extreme. This worrying development, called climate change, poses a threat to millions of people. Unexpected events such as severe drought, a dramatic increase in flooding, or an unusually severe winter affect not only food production, but also human life itself. Once more, it is those who are already living on the edge of survival who are most vulnerable.

Getting Warmer

The impact of the changing climate is more extreme in places where poverty and hunger are greatest. A warming planet brings disruption to the food chain on land and in the oceans. Thousands of animals in the sea depend on coral for food and shelter. Coral is a rocky seabed deposit made from the skeletons of millions of tiny creatures. Coral is particularly vulnerable to the higher levels of ultra violet light from the Sun caused by the thinning of the ozone layer in Earth's atmosphere. As the Sun's rays bleach the coral, it dies, breaking a vital link in the food chain. On land, increasingly mild winters mean that pests are not killed off, so more locusts, aphids, and other destructive insects survive to attack and damage crops in greater numbers.

A Plague of Locusts

Every year around the world, locusts cause crop damage costing millions of dollars. When heavy summer rainfall is followed by dry, warm weather, female locusts may lay three times as many eggs as usual in the soil. In the past, the soil was plowed before seeds were sown, exposing the eggs to the air so they dried out and died. However, farmers now use a technique of direct drilling to sow seeds. It is quicker and cheaper than traditional methods but also means that millions of locust eggs survive to hatch and destroy crops.

SCIENCE SOLUTIONS

New Pest Controls

Farmers in Australia use aircraft to spray strong chemical compounds, called insecticides, on farmland to kill off pests such as locusts. The problem is that these chemicals can pollute water supplies and cause illnesses in humans. However, biologists have discovered that locusts are naturally allergic to a species of fungus called Metarhizium. Currently, products based on the fungus are less effective and more expensive than other pest-killing treatments—but progress is being made. In the future it may be possible to use Metarhizium to control locusts and other pests, and to avoid the problems caused by chemical pest control.

CHAPTER THREE

The Hungry Millions

In developed countries, people can expect to live beyond the age of 70. In hunger-affected African countries such as Gambia and Burkina Faso, few people reach 55. There are many short-term, quick fixes for hunger problems in developing countries, such as sending food parcels or handing out high-energy biscuits. However, longer-term answers are needed to solve the hunger problem for good.

The Wider Hunger Legacy

Hunger is not restricted to people in developing countries that have to endure poor harvests or frequent wars. The areas of the world worst hit by famine and hunger are often those places that suffer a disaster such as a hurricane or an earthquake. In 2005, Hurricane Katrina struck New Orleans, and a huge food aid effort followed,

Thousands of people all over the world require long-term food aid. War, natural disasters, and crop failure are just some of the reasons for this.

carrying on for at least 12 months after the storm. The 2010 earthquake in Haiti resulted in one of the largest relief operations ever mounted. Today, Haitians are still receiving food aid and living in temporary shelters as the country is slowly rebuilt.

Across the developed world, many people visit food banks to feed their families as a result of the global economic meltdown that began in 2008. Both man-made and natural disasters add to the number of the hungry worldwide.

Volunteers collect food donations and pack them to send to those in need.

LOOK TO THE PAST

In the 1930s, during the economic crisis known as the Great Depression, the United States suffered one of its worst periods of hunger. Along with the economic problems, some disastrous farming decisions left millions of people starving. Early in the decade, a severe drought hit the flat, fertile Great Plains region, which covers approximately 500,000 square miles (1,300,000 square kilometers). Years of intensive farming had left the topsoil loose and powdery. Plowing had removed the natural grasses, so that when powerful winds came there was nothing to hold the soil to the ground. Enormous black dust clouds swept across the land, destroying crops, homes, and livelihoods. The destruction taught farmers valuable lessons, and farming methods across the United States changed. Soil protection became the number one priority. Today, people in other parts of the world are also learning to allow soil to recover by alternating the crops grown on a piece of land from year to year and not planting it at all every few years.

Famine and Families

According to the hunger-relief organization the WFP, in the time it takes to read this sentence a child will have died from hunger. Every year, 7 million children die from preventable hunger, a number that will rise with continuing water shortages and soil depletion in many parts of the developing world. For some children, it is already too late to be saved. For others, time is quickly running out.

Hunger and Families

The effect of hunger and malnutrition on families is terrible. In developing countries, fathers often travel far away from home in search of work, leaving women and children behind at home. Children are often sent out to beg for food, and women are forced to work for very little pay in order to feed their families. The food they can afford to buy is low in nutrition. The water they use for drinking and cooking is polluted. Due to their poor diet, women and children often become weaker, and ill health sets in. If the fathers cannot find work and send home money, the situation quickly becomes desperate.

In developing countries, parents are often forced to move away from their families to look for work in order to support them.

An Impossible Task?

Hunger and famine are highly complex problems. To deal with the crisis, governments must first buy food. Then, they must ensure there is an organized transportation system to distribute the food. Finally, governments need to make sure that food supplies are not disrupted by corruption or mismanagement. This last hurdle is often the biggest challenge of all.

SCIENCE SOLUTIONS

Nutrient Cure

Many children who suffer from poor nutrition were already malnourished even before birth. Their mothers' poor diets meant that they did not receive adequate nourishment in the uterus for proper growth and development. Low nutrition during a woman's pregnancy can cause a baby to be born with a low birth weight, which, in turn, can lead to learning disabilities, poor health, and even death. Malnourished children are more prone to illnesses such as diarrhea and diseases like malaria, pneumonia, and measles. This is because their bodies are too weak to use the food they do eat to fight against disease. Medical research shows that the three most important nutrients for maintaining good health are Vitamin A, iron, and iodine. Giving malnourished children these nutrients could protect them from blindness, anemia, and mental health problems.

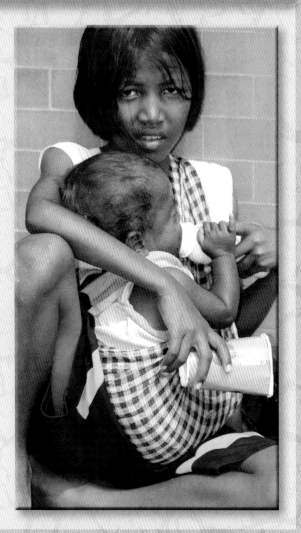

Hunger on the Rise

The UN estimates that 15 percent of people in the developing world are currently hungry, compared with less than 1 percent across the developed countries. However, hunger is also increasing in developed countries as a result of global economic problems. One of the countries worst affected by economic troubles is Greece, where 90 percent of the people in poor neighborhoods rely on soup kitchens and food banks. Nearly 600,000 Greek children are hungry, often surviving on as little as just one meal each day.

A Lack of Nourishment

From mountain villages in Bolivia, South America, to the shanty towns of Johannesburg, South Africa, undernourishment is rising at a frightening rate. It is impossible to calculate the exact number of people around the world who are undernourished, but it is a problem that crosses borders, cultures, and economic boundaries. Women who are undernourished cannot breast-feed their babies. Growing children who are undernourished do not develop healthy bodies and minds. Low levels of nutrition mean that children find it difficult to concentrate in school. They also find it difficult to play, and even sleep.

The young and the elderly are often the first to suffer hunger. This Greek woman is begging for food for herself and her child.

In Burkina Faso, Africa, finding enough food to eat is a daily struggle for many families.

Food Banks

Across the developed world, food banks are lifelines for families struggling to meet rising food costs. In the United States, almost 50 million people live in households that are described as "food insecure." This means that there is no fixed or regular household income, so there is not always enough food. The worst affected states are Mississippi, Arkansas, and Texas, and the numbers of hungry families there are rising.

COUNTDOWN!

In 1980, there were approximately 4.5 billion people on Earth; by 2013, there were an estimated 7 billion, a number that is rising quickly. Most adults need around 2,000 to 2,500 calories per day for good health. Scientists have calculated that the world's farmers produce enough food to feed the planet's population. The problem is that most of this food is grown and consumed in developed countries. Many people in the world do not have enough land to grow, or money to buy, sufficient food. Crossing borders to distribute the world's food to those who do not have enough is now the key focus for governments and for the FAO.

Many people are forced to leave their homes to search for work and food. The Dadaab refugee camp in Somalia is home to thousands of hungry people.

The Effects of Hunger

One of the worst effects of hunger is even more hunger, continuing from one generation to the next, without any hope of change. Hunger also creates more poverty and affects people's health, intellectual development, and future potential.

Crucial Early Years

Doctors know that the first two years of a child's life are crucial in terms of his or her long-term health. A child who is undernourished during this period will not get the essential vitamins and minerals that come from a healthy, balanced diet. This can lead to permanent damage to bones and organs and, at its most extreme, result in stunted growth and a lifetime of ill health. A lack of nutrition can affect a child's intellectual development and academic performance. It can also mean earning a lower wage later in life, so the cycle of poverty and undernourishment continues into the next generation.

Living with Hunger

Hunger affects not only physical health, but also overall well-being. Consider how you feel when you are hungry. Do you feel irritable, tired, or even sad? People who are permanently undernourished feel all these things and more. Their energy is sapped so they cannot find work.

Their thinking processes are slow because they are concentrating simply on staying alive. Charities and organizations around the world work to give not just food to the millions of hungry people but also the hope, energy, and skills they need to lead a fulfilling life.

LOOK TO THE PAST

Sometimes, "people power" can make an enormous difference and help to change situations for the better. In the 1970s and 1980s, the African country of Ethiopia endured a series of crippling droughts. An unstable political background meant that the country suffered from an ongoing conflict, which further upset food supplies. Millions of people went hungry. In 1984, television news reports raised public awareness in Britain, and a great charity campaign was born. A music group named Band Aid was formed and the song "Do They Know It's Christmas?" was a worldwide hit. All the money raised from sales of the record was given to the Ethiopian famine appeal. The 1985 Live Aid concert that then followed was watched by millions all over the world and raised even more money. Band Aid continues to fundraise today to help victims of hunger and famine everywhere.

CHAPTER FOUR

The Race to Find Solutions

One of the best ways of fighting famine is to help people in affected areas to grow their own food. If they can improve the way they farm, then food production and harvest yields will increase and hunger will decline. However, with Earth's climate changing, new farming techniques must be found if parts of the planet are to produce enough food to feed a growing population.

China's Food Problem

China has the largest population of any country in the world—and it is growing all the time. Increasing food production has been a top priority in China for many years. However, as the country industrializes, more and more people are leaving agriculture and moving to the cities in search of better-paid work, more education, and greater opportunities. It is estimated that by 2030 China's food production will have to increase by

In Costa Rica, the need to make the land more productive means that chemical pesticides are used. This pollutes the water and has affected human health.

▼

COUNTDOWN!

Development in some developing countries has resulted in poor management of natural resources. The economy of Costa Rica in Central America relies on agriculture. To make the country's land more productive, crops have been sprayed with many tons of chemical pesticides, but these chemicals have also polluted the water and even poisoned farm workers. The race is on to find a healthy alternative that will not weaken the farming economy.

60 percent if the country is to avoid devastating famine and rocketing food prices.

One of the ways China is coping with fewer farm workers and a higher population needing more food is by grouping farms together to create "collective farms." On these farms, larger machines work a greater area of land, which makes the farms more efficient.

Africa's Challenges

Africa has the fastest-growing population rate of any continent on Earth, so the need to produce food in an efficient and sustainable way there is key to avoiding future famine. Biotechnology may hold some of the answers to making Africa self-sufficient in food production, but a lack of suitable arable land is a real challenge. Drought and conflicts have left many places in Africa infertile. The added issues of disease, pests, and inadequate rainfall have all contributed to a highly complex problem.

These refugees are totally reliant on food aid. It will take millions of dollars and a great deal of support to enable them to become self-sufficient again.

Making the Most of Water

Drought is now the single most common cause of food shortages in the world. It leads to crop failures and livestock deaths. The countries worst hit by drought are those along Earth's equator, such as Guatemala in Central America, and Somalia and Kenya in Africa. Many of these countries face the problem of sourcing and supplying enough water to irrigate farmland.

Smart Ways with Water

Hot, dry countries must find ways of making their deserts "green" through smart irrigation schemes. These schemes can turn even marginal land into fertile, productive areas. Water pumps and aqueducts have been used since ancient times to bring water from water-rich areas to drier places where it is needed for farming. Now, in Israel, engineers and inventors have come up with a system that is even more efficient. Israeli scientists have discovered that watering plants in a slow and balanced way,

SCIENCE SOLUTIONS

Creating Water

How do you make fresh water in the desert? If a country has a coastline, one way is to collect seawater and remove the salt. However, this process, called desalination, is expensive and environmentally damaging. An alternative is to use wind turbines to make water. You may have seen water dripping from an air-conditioning unit. Wind turbines use a similar process to create water. Inside the turbine is a compressor that condenses water from the air. Some turbines can produce around 260 gallons (1,000 L) of drinking water a day. Imagine a world in which thousands of wind turbines create fresh water from air—it is an environmentally friendly method that could mean the difference between a successful harvest and a disastrous famine.

known as drip irrigation, leads to amazing growth. This type of micro-irrigation is a way of saving enormous amounts of fresh water. Farmers in Senegal, Africa, are now also using this irrigation method to improve their harvests.

Israeli farmers have found another smart way to save water and transform infertile desert into farmland. They simply use the natural moisture in the air. During the night, that moisture forms small drops of water, called dew, on cool surfaces. The farmers use plastic trays placed around their plants to collect the dew, which, it is estimated, can provide 50 percent of the water a tree or plant needs.

Even in a hot, dry country such as Israel, smart irrigation schemes mean that agriculture can be successful.

Education and Equality

One of the key ways in which the cycle of poverty can be stopped is through education. In many parts of the world, education rates are poor, limiting people's opportunities and inhibiting their ability to earn money and feed their families. It is often said that if you educate a woman, you educate a family, so there are many schemes in developing countries that focus on women and girls.

For these children in Hyderabad, Pakistan, education is the best way to improve their lives, by offering opportunities and good nutrition.

Education in the Andes

Peru is a vast, mountainous country in South America where most people live far away from major towns and cities. These people survive by small-scale farming and rearing a few animals. Going to school often means walking for more than an hour through the mountains, a journey that can be dangerous in the dark. This is a great barrier to education and means that many children, particularly girls, drop out of school. Nearly half of rural Peruvian children do not go to school, and of those who do, less than half complete their education. This traps the children and, when they become adults, their families in poverty and inequality. It is a pattern seen in many parts of the world.

Almost half of rural Peruvian children do not go to school. As a result, they are trapped in a cycle of low education, poverty, and hunger.

Changing Times in Africa

Liberia is a developing African nation that has been devastated by years of civil war. As a result, the vast majority of the population lives in poverty. Fighting has displaced many thousands of people, and schooling has been severely disrupted. In the few places where education is available, the priority for families is educating boys. Currently, the majority of Liberian teachers are unqualified, and less than 20 percent are female. The UN is working with the Liberian government and charities to ensure that more Liberian girls receive a basic education. This should improve their earning potential as adults and reduce their chances of falling into poverty.

LOOK TO THE PAST

Ellen Johnson Sirleaf is the president of Liberia and the first woman to be elected leader of an African country. Her family comes from humble beginnings. Both her parents were born into poverty, but through education they were able to change their family's fortunes. Sirleaf herself studied economics and accounting and then continued her studies in the United States. In 2011, Sirleaf won the Nobel Peace Prize for her work on women's rights, fair government, and improving social justice. She is an example of how education can create opportunity and change lives.

Science to the Rescue?

Consider how much food you eat every day. Then think about how much your family consumes each week. If that seems a lot, imagine how much food is needed to feed 7 billion people. Is it really possible to feed that many people? Many scientists think that it is, but only if we change how we farm and how we use technology, and if we refocus our efforts on protecting the environment.

Robot Workers

The next time you travel past a farm, greenhouse, or orchard, look closely—you might see a robot! A European project is creating robots to harvest high-value crops such as orchard fruits, grapes, and vegetables in polytunnels. The robots are programmed to spray selected targets and to harvest only the ripe products, thereby producing less food waste. It is estimated that the project will have commercial potential within around five years and could be one of the answers to sustainable food production.

The Super Potato!

Microbiology is at the cutting edge of food production, and Israeli Professor David Levy has developed a very smart foodstuff indeed—the

Scientists are working with farmers to discover how vegetables can be grown more efficiently in climate-controlled greenhouses such as this one.

super potato. This potato can adapt to the extreme heat and dryness of the Middle East and can also be irrigated with seawater. Plant biologists from other regions of the world with similar climatic conditions, such as North Africa, are already trialing the super potato. The potential impact of this new vegetable on poverty and hunger is enormous and far-reaching.

Biotech Bananas

In Uganda, Africa, biotechnology is helping to not only increase production of bananas, potatoes, and sugarcane, but also to improve their vitamin content. More than 50 percent of children under the age of five in Uganda suffer from Vitamin A deficiency, which can lead to stunted growth. However, within the next few years, Ugandan farmers will be growing bananas with six times the normal level of Vitamin A as a result of biotechnology.

SCIENCE SOLUTIONS

Bug Resistant

All over the world, farmers use pesticides and fertilizers to protect and nurture their crops. However, because of environmental and health concerns, the development of new chemical treatments has declined in recent years. Scientists are now altering the chemical makeup of plants to make them more resistant to bugs. This could be a solution to food shortages in parts of the word, such as India, with high population growth. India must double its food production by 2040 if the country is to feed its people.

By improving the vitamin content of bananas, fewer children will suffer from Vitamin A deficiency. This use of biotechnology could help children in banana-growing countries such as Uganda.

Farm the Desert

It sounds crazy, but desert farms are a brilliantly simple solution to food and water shortages in some hot countries. With climate change destroying soil quality in many parts of the world, more land is becoming infertile desert. Rather than waste vast amounts of precious freshwater trying to fight a losing battle against nature, scientists have designed special greenhouses just for desert conditions. The greenhouses are built in desert areas near coasts. Seawater is pumped into the building and turned into freshwater through evaporation. The freshwater is then used to water the plants.

COUNTDOWN!

By 2050, it is estimated that the Earth's population will be an incredible 9 billion. This will put a huge strain on the planet's food and water supplies. Globally, there are already nearly 1 billion people suffering from hunger so the race to find solutions is on.

Sat-nav Soil Sensors

Scientists in the United States have found an answer to two key farming problems: water waste and poor harvests. Small sensors are buried in the earth to measure moisture and nutrient levels. This information is then transmitted to a computer, and global positioning system- (GPS-) guided tractors add water or fertilizer only where and when it is required. This type of precision farming can double harvests, reduce water waste, and could be happening in a field near you within just five years.

Scientists are studying plant growth in artificial biomes, such as Biosphere 2 (left) in Arizona, to understand how best to farm crops in artificial conditions.

Scientists are working hard to create genetically modified supercrops, such as this crop of maize, in the hope that such foods could feed Earth's growing population. Some people believe that genetically modified foods have not yet been proven safe to eat, so scientists and governments will need to work hard to persuade people that supercrops are the future.

Changing Nature

With a super-sized global population set to grow even larger, scientists are searching for a new breed of supercrops. Supercrops are plants such as wheat or rice, which are altered to make them more pest-resistant or fruitful. With the clock already ticking, genetically modified foods could be the answer to the world's food shortage.

More than half of the global population depends on rice as part of its diet, but rice does not grow everywhere. It also grows quite slowly, with just one harvest per year. Experts predict that China and India will experience the largest rise in population over the next 50 years, so much more rice will be needed to avoid large-scale famine in these countries.

Plant Science

Scientists at the International Rice Research Institute in the Philippines have altered the chemical structure of rice so that it uses the Sun's energy differently and grows much faster. They are also trying to genetically modify the rice plant so that it will grow in areas where famine already exists, such as sub-Saharan Africa. More tests need to be carried out, but super-rice could be a reality within 10 years.

CHAPTER FIVE

Future Hopes and Challenges

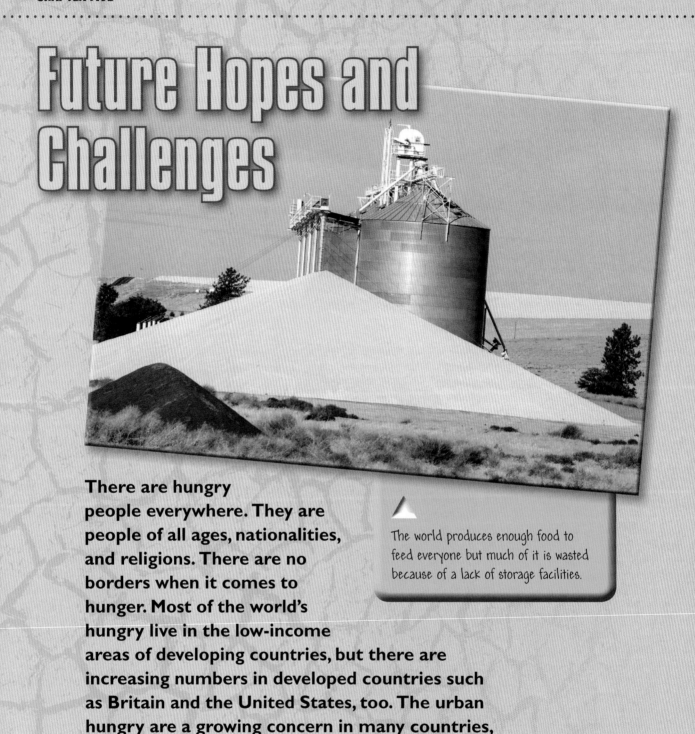

The world produces enough food to feed everyone but much of it is wasted because of a lack of storage facilities.

There are hungry people everywhere. They are people of all ages, nationalities, and religions. There are no borders when it comes to hunger. Most of the world's hungry live in the low-income areas of developing countries, but there are increasing numbers in developed countries such as Britain and the United States, too. The urban hungry are a growing concern in many countries, particularly as more people migrate to cities to look for work. There is also still the great challenge of breaking the poverty cycle through the education of everybody, not just the rich and not only boys.

Future Factors

Dealing with climate change, wars, political corruption, an ever-growing population, and high food prices are just some of the challenges facing governments today in the fight against hunger. Food security, sustainable farming, and efficient water use are also extremely important in making sure everyone has enough to eat. More than 60 percent of the hungriest people live in Asia, so a fairer distribution of the world's food is vital. Some countries have tried to become food independent too quickly and have damaged soil by using too many chemical fertilizers. The UN works closely with developed and developing nations to try to find solutions to all these serious and complex problems.

LOOK TO THE PAST

In Britain in the late eighteenth and early nineteenth centuries, there was mass migration from the countryside to the towns. People believed that it would be better for work and for their families. When people arrived in the industrial factory towns, they had to live in squalid conditions. Often, one family would live in a single room and share toilet facilities with perhaps five other families. The wages people earned were also not as high as they had expected, and workers were often paid in tokens that could be spent only in factory-owned stores. Quickly, the workers' houses became slums, and hunger and disease were rife. Now, history is repeating itself with mass urbanization across Asia, Africa, and South America. Today's shanty towns of South America and Africa have the same problems as those seen in nineteenth-century Britain—poverty, hunger, overcrowding, and disease.

The Zero Hunger Challenge

How can we ensure everyone in the world has enough to eat? Which solutions are the best and most effective? Charity and aid are the short-term answers, for example, members of Chabad gave food to poor Jewish families on September 15, 2008, in Sderot, Israel. Chabad is an organization that aims to help all Jewish people. However, if hunger is to be wiped out, far more needs to be done.

One Country, One Solution

In 2003, the government of Brazil created the Zero Hunger program with the aim of ending hunger and extreme poverty in that country. The program guarantees all Brazilian people the right to basic food and clean water. Education programs about healthy eating have also been run alongside the widespread distribution of vitamin and iron supplements. Children who attend school get a free meal at lunchtime. Within the first 10 years of the program, more children were both going to and staying in school. Literacy rates have risen and, slowly but surely, the number of hungry people in Brazil is decreasing.

Ongoing Threat

Hunger remains a bigger threat to life than the diseases HIV/AIDS, malaria, and tuberculosis combined. Globally, one in eight people cannot lead a healthy and active life because they have too little food. The key cause of hunger is poverty. In turn, hunger leads to poverty, which traps millions in a deadly cycle.

Chabad is a Jewish food and educational organization. Here, Chabad volunteers hand out food aid to poor Jewish families in Israel.

A Day to Remember

Every year on October 16, World Food
Day takes place. The purpose of the day
is to raise awareness of the scale of the
global hunger problem. Chronic hunger
is with us all the time and often takes
second place to the short-term hunger
victims of natural disasters such as floods,
tsunamis, or earthquakes. Too many
people do not have enough food for
their basic physical needs and mental
development. World Food Day organizes
projects and programs all over the
world to help people become self-
reliant, to produce their own food, and
to live their lives with a sense of hope.

Sadly, it is often the youngest and most
vulnerable members of society that are
most greatly affected by hunger.

COUNTDOWN!

The UN calculates that the number of hungry people in
the world could be reduced by 150 million if women farmers had the
same access to tools, seeds, and land as men. Around the world, women
grow more food than men, but the cultural and social traditions in many
hunger hot spots mean that women are affected more by hunger than
men. Cultures tend to change very slowly, but if more women are going
to get out of the poverty and hunger trap, change needs to happen now.

▲ Scientists are making advances in biotechnology all the time. This could be the best answer to the problem of feeding the world's population.

Can We Win the Race?

There are many governments, organizations, and charities that are committed to helping the world's hungry and bringing about an end to famine and poverty. The UN, the WFP, and the World Bank work closely with organizations such as Save the Children, Oxfam, and Make Poverty History to change things for the better. If we work as a global society, change is possible and hunger can become a thing of the past. However, hunger is a highly complex problem, involving often controversial areas such as education, economics, culture, and climate change.

A Fair Way to Trade

Small-scale farmers in developing countries rely on being able to sell their produce for a fair price. The UN is working with governments to organize fair trade deals to ensure richer countries pay the farmers a fair price for their food and not demand it too cheaply. By doing so, the deal is a good one for the farmers and they can start to farm and trade their way out of poverty.

What Can We Do?

We can all play our part in helping to stop hunger. Raising awareness and raising money for charities and aid organizations are things most people can do. You can also help by buying goods marked with the Fairtrade logo. By doing so, you know that your money is going directly to those who need it most.

COUNTDOWN!

If the ultimate goal of zero hunger is to be achieved, governments all over the world need to work together to help the people who are most affected. One of the biggest challenges for governments is producing enough food for growing populations, but using less land and fewer chemicals. Developed nations need to help countries with high hunger rates to create roads and railroads to transport food quickly and safely.

Developing nations also need help with education programs and farming techniques. The biggest need of all, however, is to make sure that the millions of men, women, and children all over the world who are going hungry today will get food tomorrow. Their survival clock is ticking, and the time to help save them is running out.

Glossary

HIV/AIDS A disease that attacks the immune system.

anemia A blood condition caused by low iron levels.

aphid An insect that feeds on plants.

aqueduct A bridge that carries water.

arable Used for growing crops, usually land.

austerity A government policy of reducing public spending in order to reduce a country's debt.

biofortification Strengthening nutrients in plants artificially.

biotechnology The manipulation of living things to create new products, such as genetically modified (GM) crops.

chronic hunger Long-term hunger.

corruption Dishonesty for personal gain.

displace To force somebody to leave his or her home.

drought A period of time when there is little or no rain.

epidemic A fast-spreading disease.

food bank Emergency food service.

genetically modified (GM) To artificially change the chemical structure of a plant (or animal).

Global Positioning System (GPS) A satellite navigation system.

immune system The human body's way of combating disease.

impairment The weakening of something.

infrastructure A network of resources, such as power and transportation, that allows a country to function.

irrigate To water.

malnutrition Without healthy food.

monocropping To grow only one crop.

nutrient Nourishing substance.

polytunnels Long greenhouses made of plastic.

poverty line The level of income below which a person is considered to be poor.

refugee Someone forced from his or her own country and seeking a safe place to live.

scheme A plan or a way of doing something.

self-sufficient Able to look after oneself.

shanty town An urban slum.

social justice Fairness for everyone.

soil depletion The process of soil becoming infertile.

soup kitchen A charity café where free food is given out.

squalid Dirty and unhygienic.

sustainable Maintaining the environmental balance.

ultra violet Harmful light from the Sun.

urban Town or city areas.

yield The amount of crops harvested from a farm.

Further Reading

Books

Anderson, Judith. *Ending Poverty and Hunger* (Working for Our Future). North Mankato, MN: Sea to Sea Publications, 2010.

Cunningham, Kevin. *Surviving Droughts and Famines* (Children's True Stories: Natural Disasters). North Mankato, MN: Raintree, 2011.

Langley, Andrew. *Avoiding Hunger and Finding Water* (Raintree Freestyle: the Environment Challenge). North Mankato, MN: Raintree, 2011.

O'Neill, Joseph R. *The Irish Potato Famine* (Essential Events). Minneapolis, MN: ABDO, 2009.

Web Sites

Due to the changing nature of Internet links, Rosen Publishing has developed an online list of Web sites related to the subject of this book. This site is updated regularly. Please use this link to access the list:

http://www.rosenlinks.com/WIC/Hung

Index